Contents Part 1

Name: ____ ___

Contents Part 2

1 Small letters

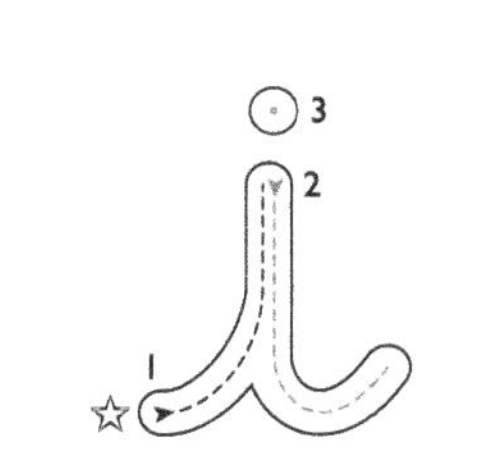

Write over each _i_ on the line here.
Start at the ☆.

Now practise writing the letter _i_ .

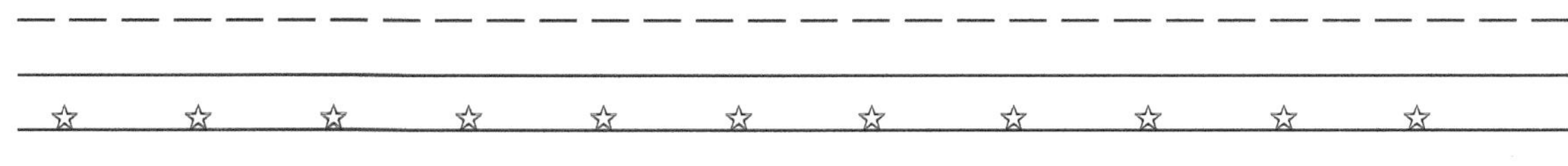

How many times is _i_ used in the sentence?

Practise writing over the letter _i_ in these words.

in is it ill dip mini

in is it ill dip mini

2 Small letters

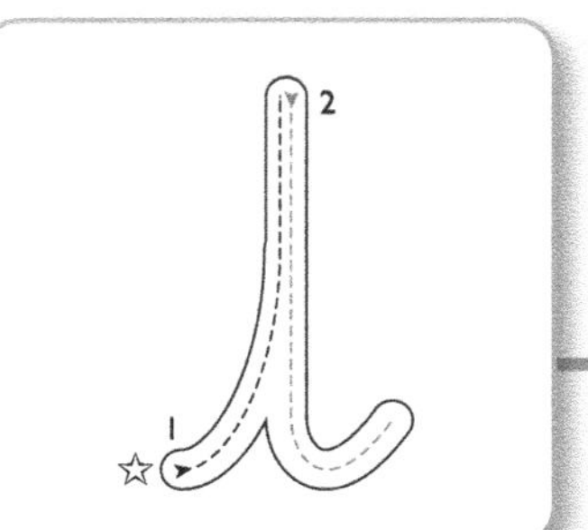

Write over each l on the line here.
Start at the ☆.

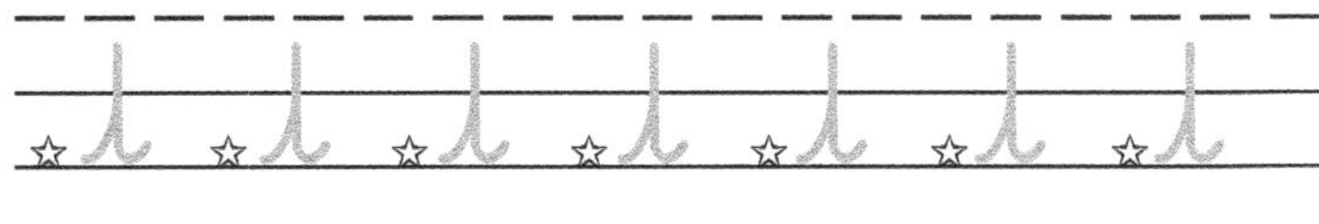

Now practise writing the letter l .

All lions like to lunch.

How many times is l used in the sentence?

Practise writing over the letter l in these words.

leg lip little ball fell

leg lip little ball fell

3 Small letters

Write over each _t_ on the line here.
Start at the ☆.

Now practise writing the letter _t_.

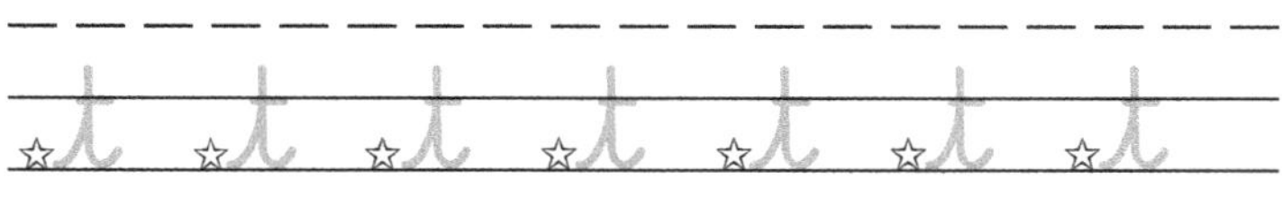

Tom tries trampolining.

How many times is _t_ used in the sentence?

Practise writing over the letter _t_ in these words.

tip try two tall attic get

tip try two tall attic get

4 Small letters

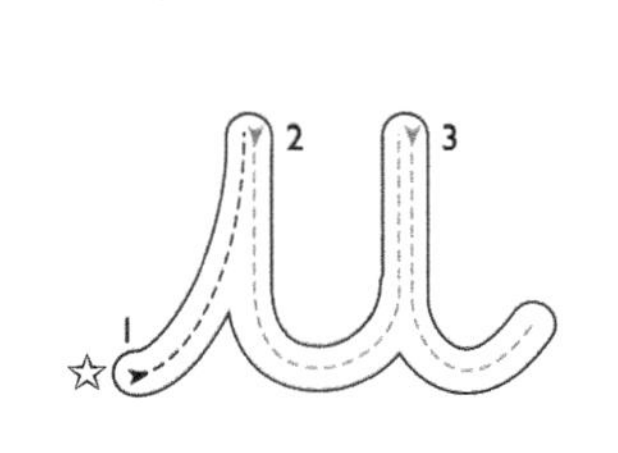

Write over each u on the line here.
Start at the ☆.

Now practise writing the letter u.

Huddle under the umbrella.

How many times is u used in the sentence? 

Practise writing over the letter u in these words.

up us under cup run

up us under cup run

5 Small letters

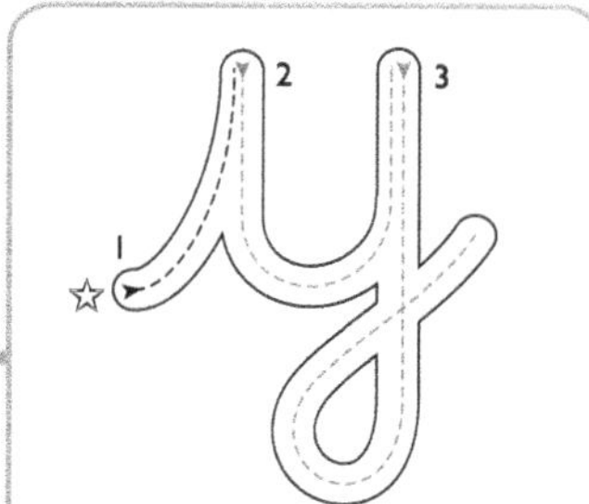

Write over each _y_ on the line here.
Start at the ☆.

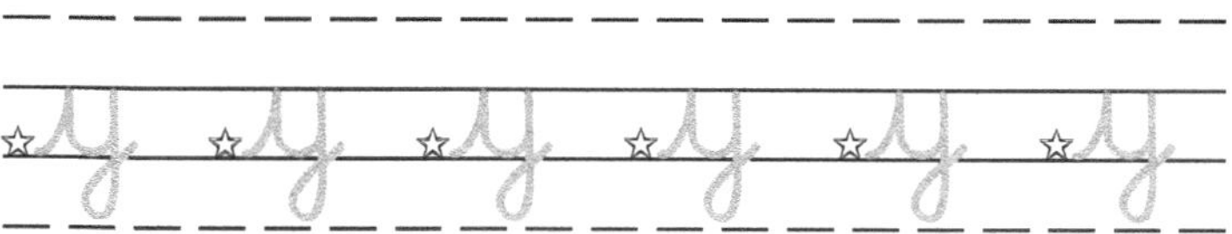

Now practise writing the letter _y_ .

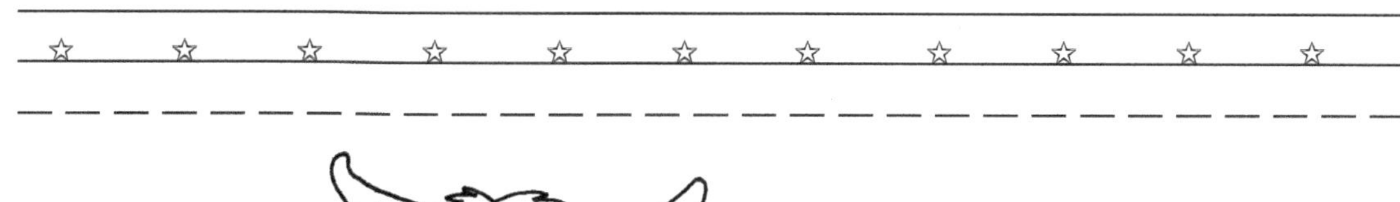

How many times is _y_ used in the sentence?

Practise writing over the letter _y_ in these words.

you   yo-yo   eye   fly   my

6 Small letters

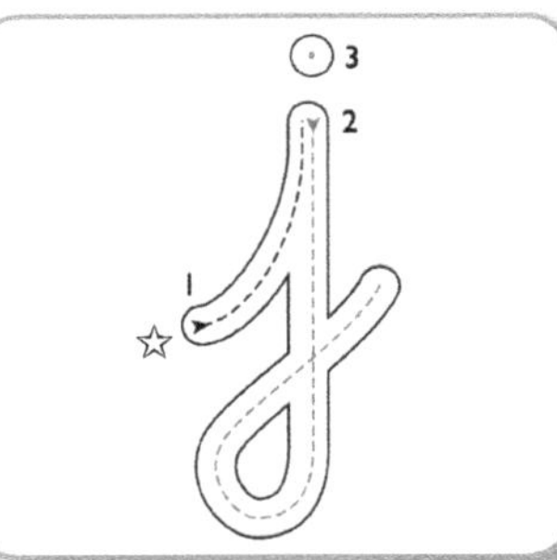

Write over each *j* on the line here.
Start at the ☆.

Now practise writing the letter *j* .

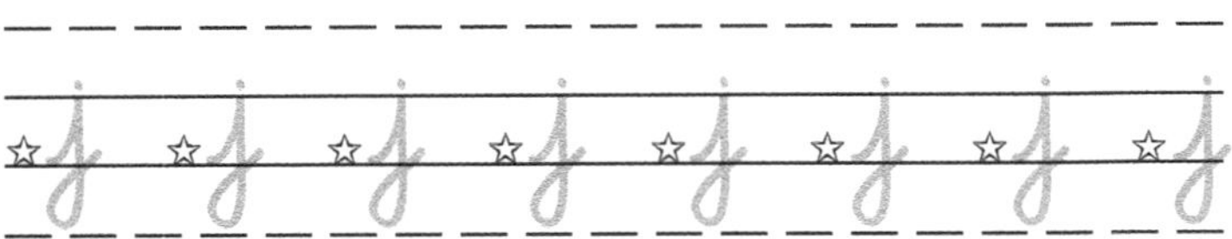

How many times is *j* used in the sentence? 

Practise writing over the letter *j* in these words.

jig jug joke jump enjoy

jig jug joke jump enjoy

Practising small letters

Write each of the letters on the three lines below.
Start at the ☆.

Now practise writing the three letters again by writing over the grey letters in each of the words below.

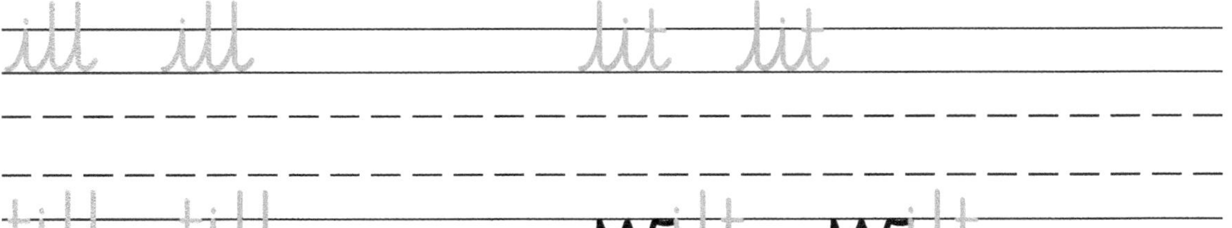

Practising small letters

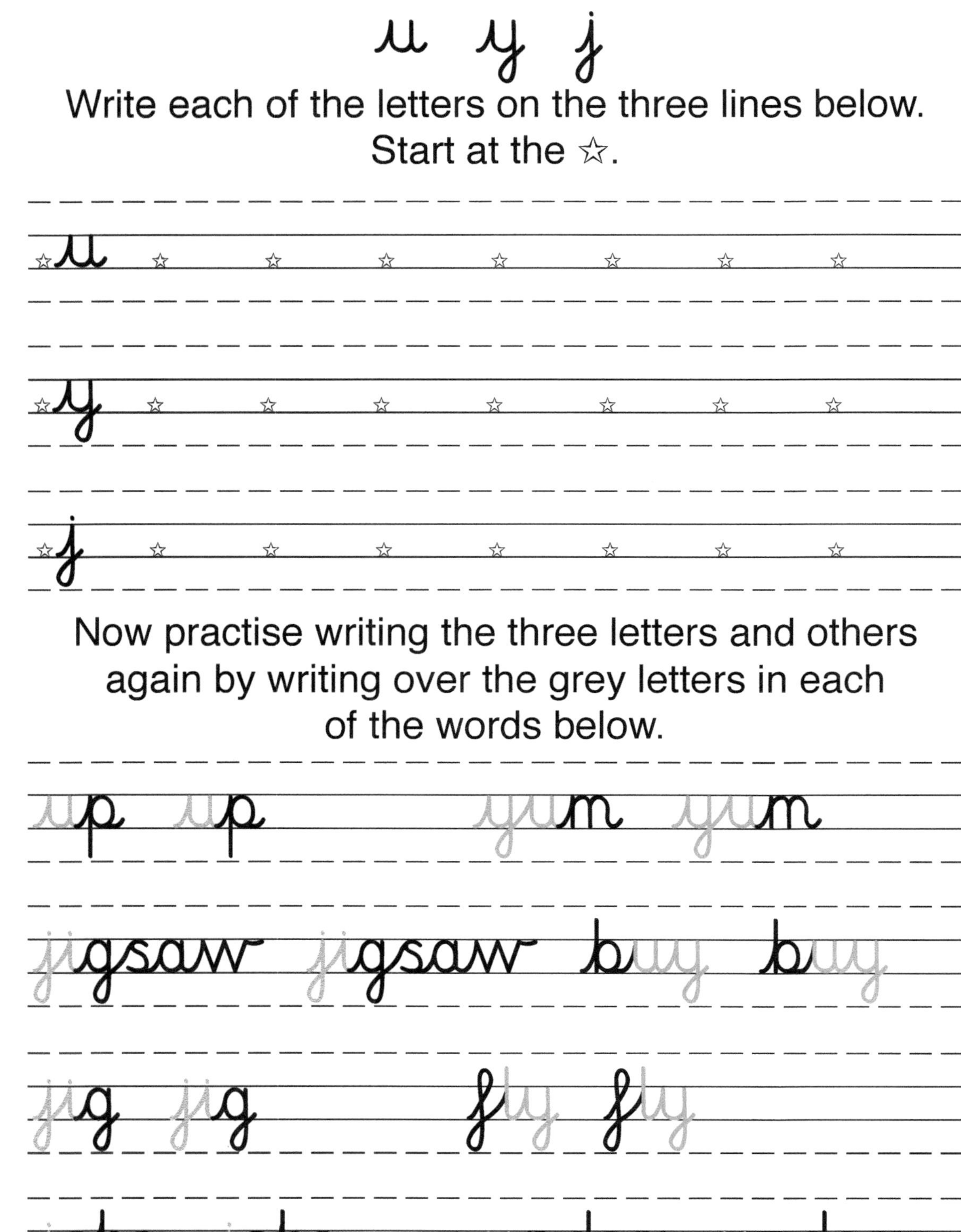

u   y   j

Write each of the letters on the three lines below.
Start at the ☆.

Now practise writing the three letters and others
again by writing over the grey letters in each
of the words below.

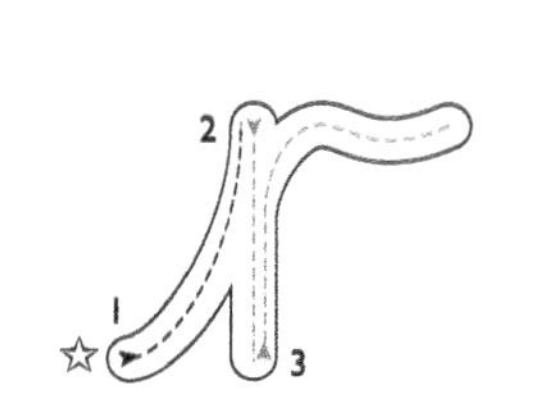

9 Small letters

Write over each r on the line here.
Start at the ☆.

☆r ☆r ☆r ☆r ☆r ☆r ☆r

Now practise writing the letter r.

☆ ☆ ☆ ☆ ☆ ☆ ☆ ☆ ☆ ☆ ☆

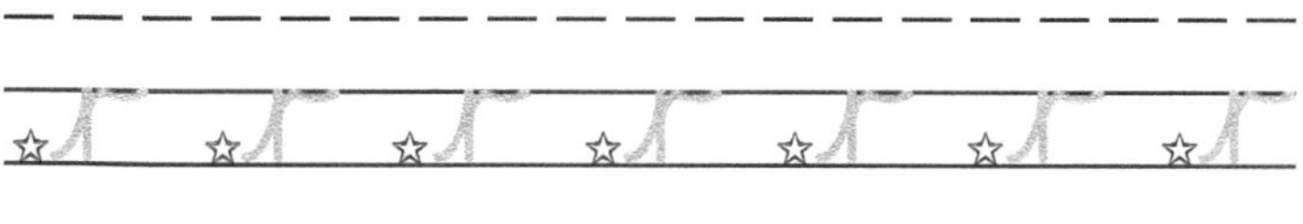

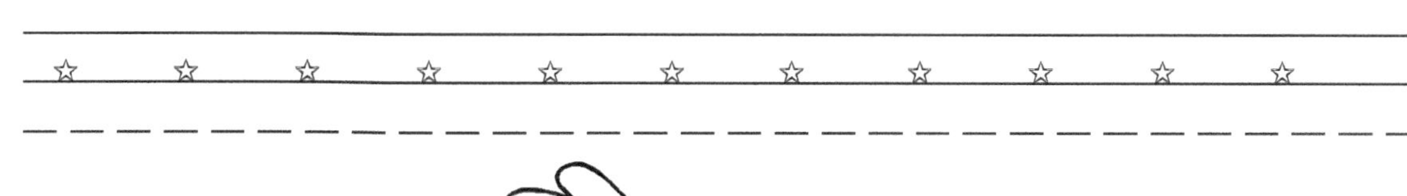

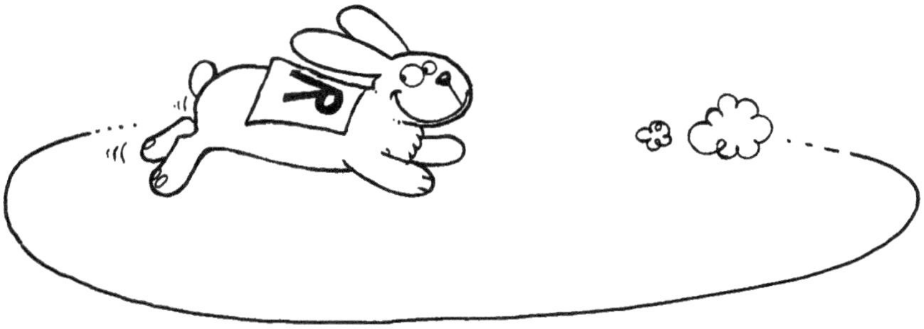

Robby rabbit runs around.

How many times is r used in the sentence? ☐

Practise writing over the letter r in these words.

rip rat roll brim car fur

rip rat roll brim car fur

Small letters

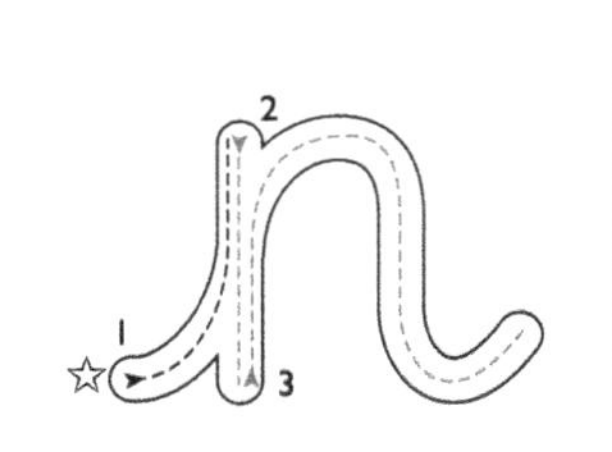

Write over each ⋀ on the line here.
Start at the ☆.

Now practise writing the letter ⋀.

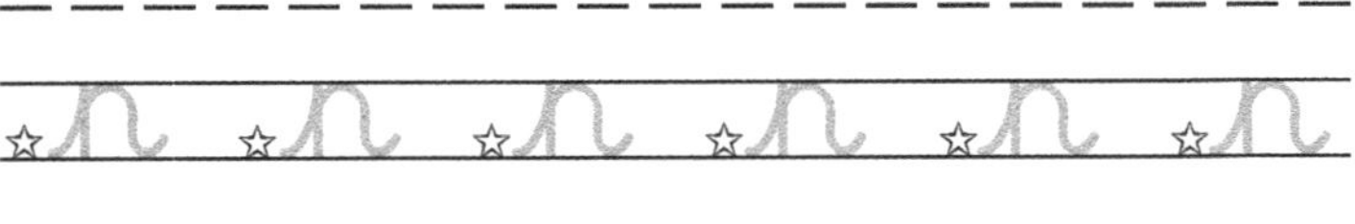

Nine hens running.

How many times is ⋀ used in the sentence?

Practise writing over the letter ⋀ in these words.

no nap not bend pin

no nap not bend pin

Small letters

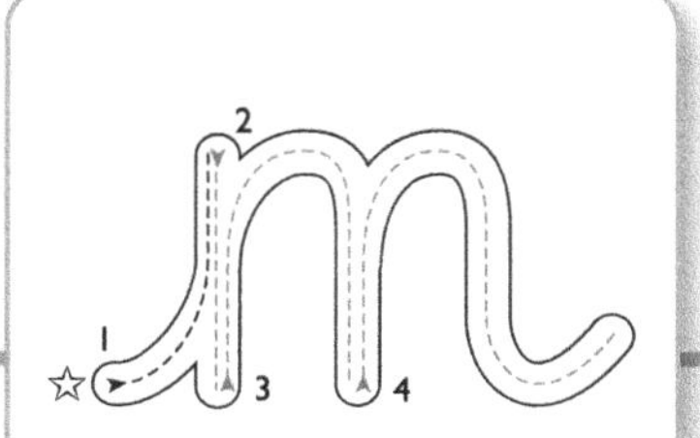

Write over each m on the line here.
Start at the ☆.

Now practise writing the letter m.

How many times is m used in the sentence?

Practise writing over the letter m in these words.

me   my   mum   lump   am

me   my   mum   lump   am

Small letters

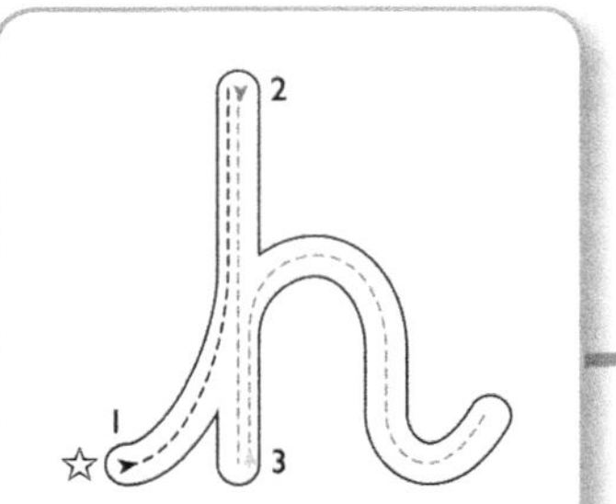

Write over each h on the line here.
Start at the ☆.

Now practise writing the letter h.

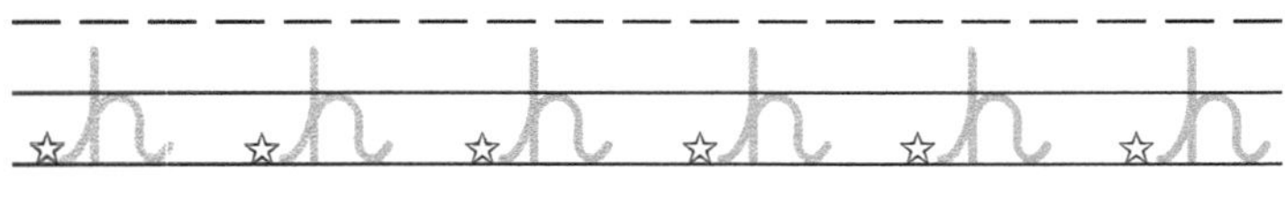

Happy horses eating hay.

How many times is h used in the sentence? 

Practise writing over the letter h in these words.

her him have chop fish

her him have chop fish

 # Small letters

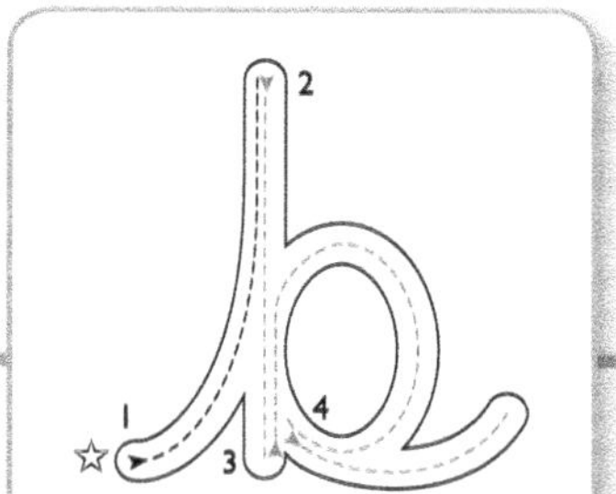

Write over each *b* on the line here.
Start at the ☆.

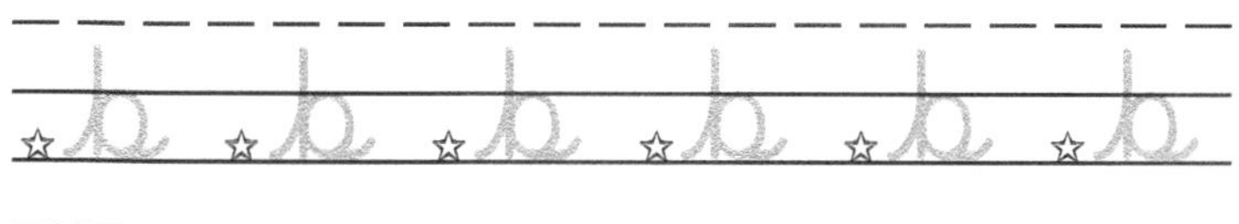

Now practise writing the letter *b* .

☆　　☆　　☆　　☆　　☆　　☆　　☆　　☆　　☆　　☆　　☆

Branches bend in the breeze.

How many times is *b* used in the sentence?

Practise writing over the letter *b* in these words.

by but bull about tub

by but bull about tub

14 | **Small letters**

Write over each *k* on the line here.
Start at the ☆.

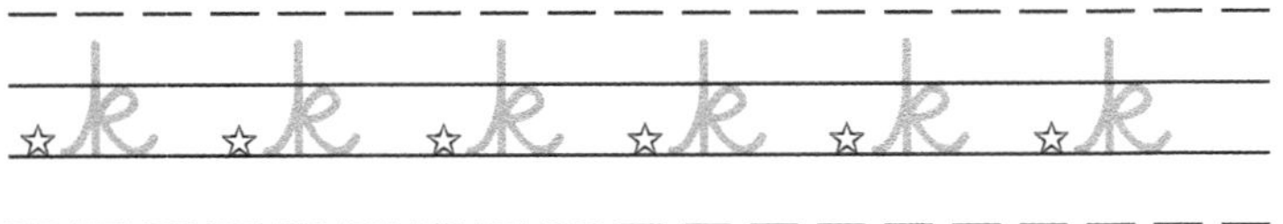

Now practise writing the letter *k*.

How many times is *k* used in the sentence? 

Practise writing over the letter *k* in these words.

keep kiss lick like tick

keep kiss lick like tick

 # Practising small letters

Write each of the letters on the three lines below.
Start at the ☆.

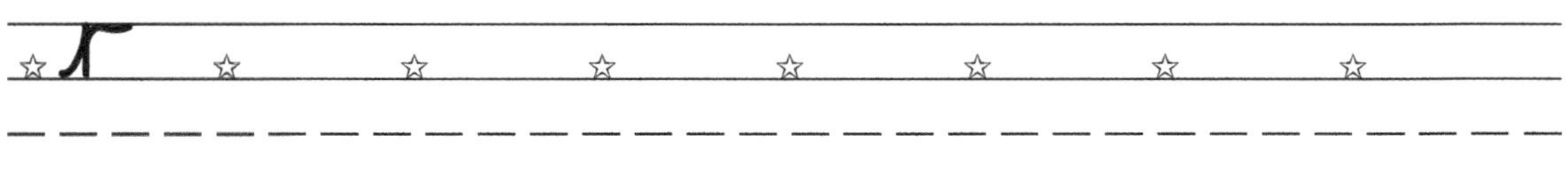

Now practise writing the three letters and others
again by writing over the grey letters in each
of the words below.

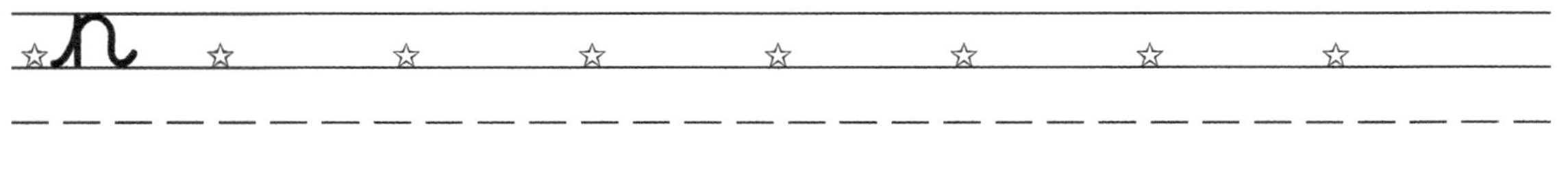

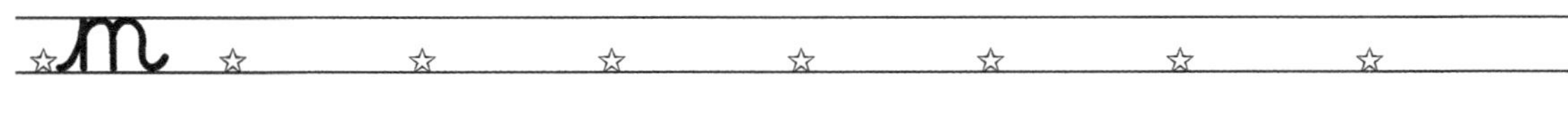

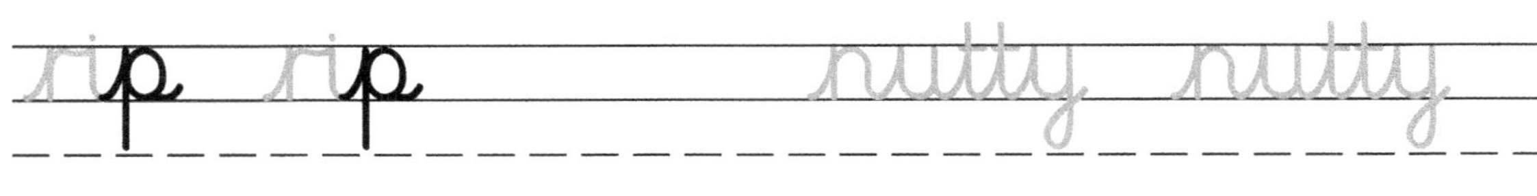

Practising small letters

Write each of the letters on the three lines below.
Start at the ☆.

Now practise writing the three letters and others
again by writing over the grey letters in each
of the words below.

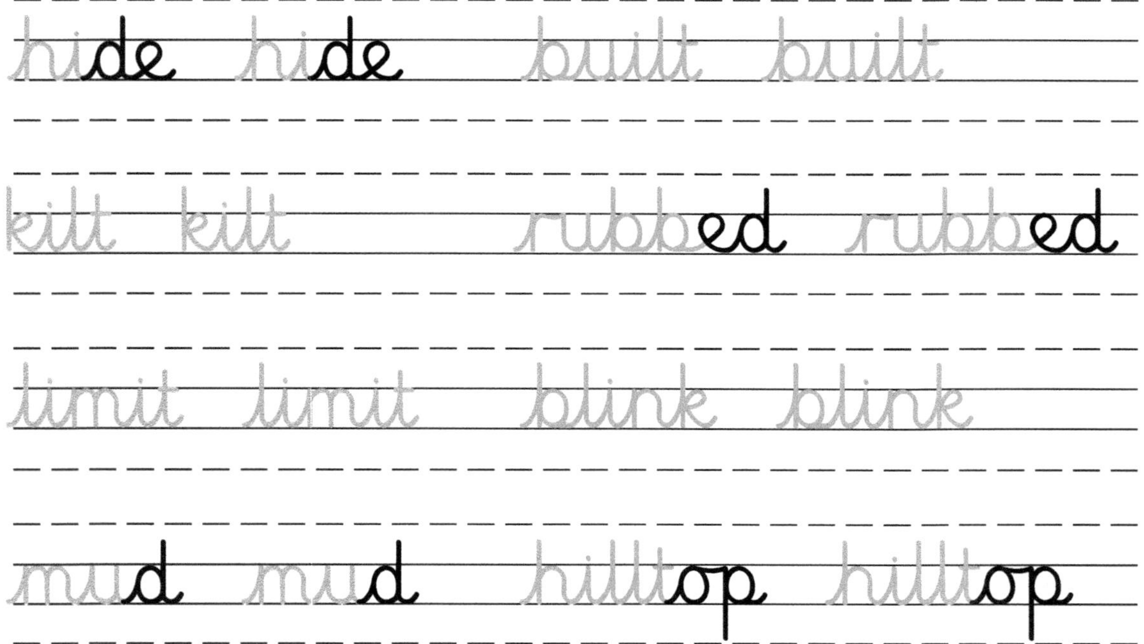

17 **Small letters**

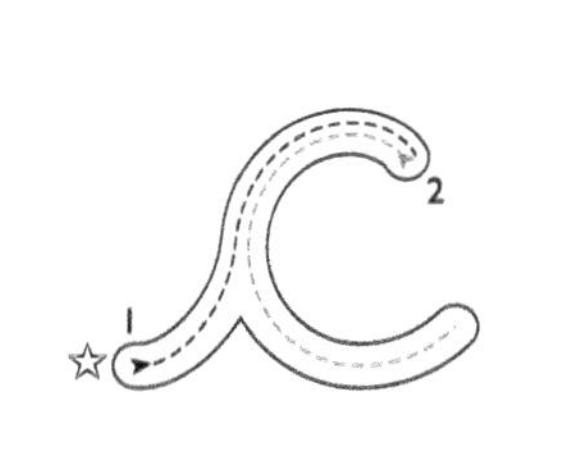

Write over each _c_ on the line here.
Start at the ☆.

Now practise writing the letter _c_ .

Count the cuddly cats.

How many times is _c_ used in the sentence?

Practise writing over the letter _c_ in these words.

cut call chick reach attic

cut call chick reach attic

 Small letters

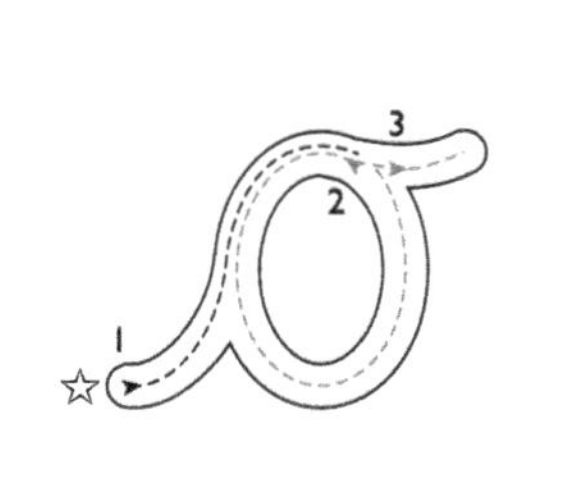

Write over each 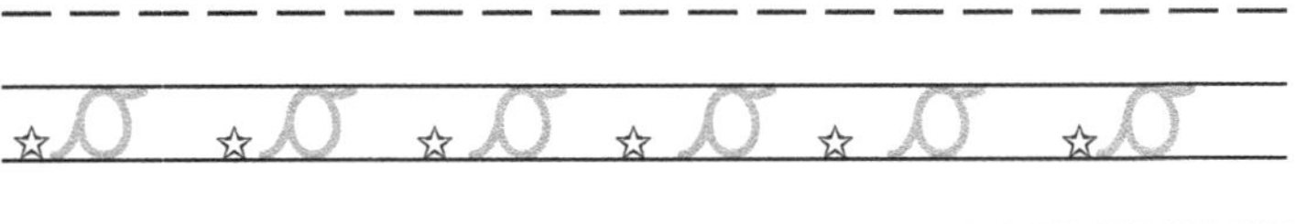 on the line here.
Start at the ☆.

Now practise writing the letter _o_ .

How many times is _o_ used in the sentence? 

Practise writing over the letter _o_ in these words.

on out over how go

on out over how go

Small letters

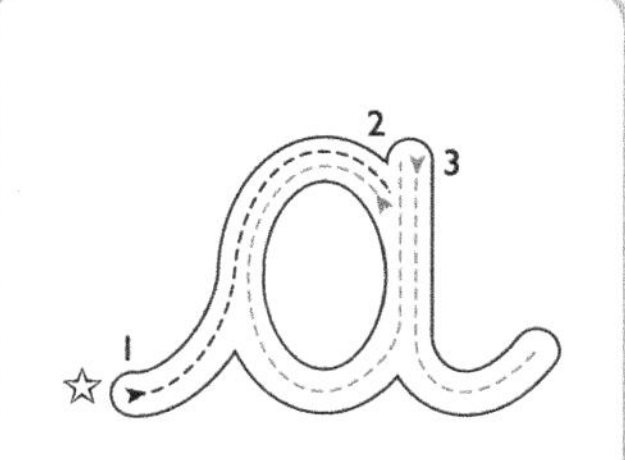

Write over each _a_ on the line here.
Start at the ☆.

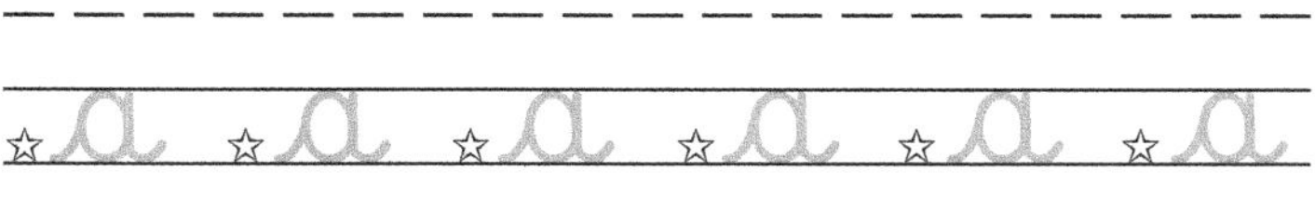

Now practise writing the letter _a_ .

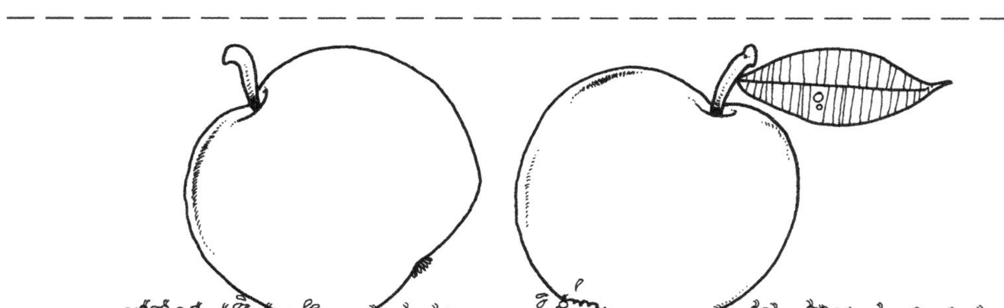

How many times is **a** used in the sentence? 

Practise writing over the letter _a_ in these words.

am as are hat back era

am as are hat back era

Small letters

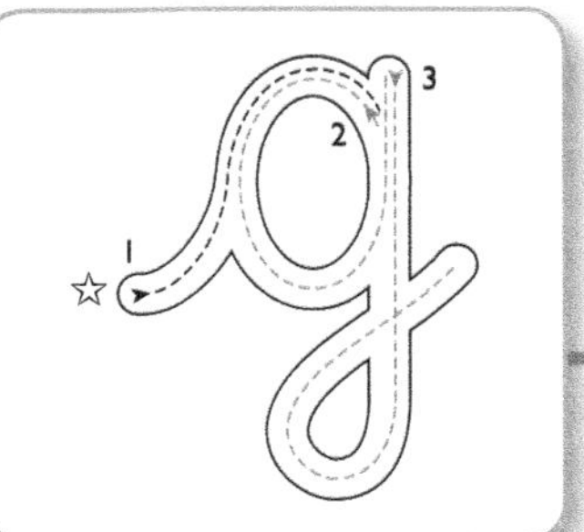

Write over each g on the line here.
Start at the ☆.

Now practise writing the letter g.

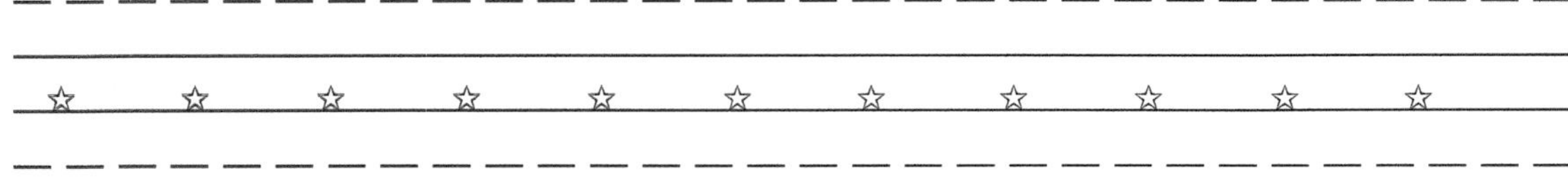

Eight bottles of gooey glue.

How many times is g used in the sentence? 

Practise writing over the letter g in these words.

go get grin age leg peg

go get grin age leg peg

Small letters

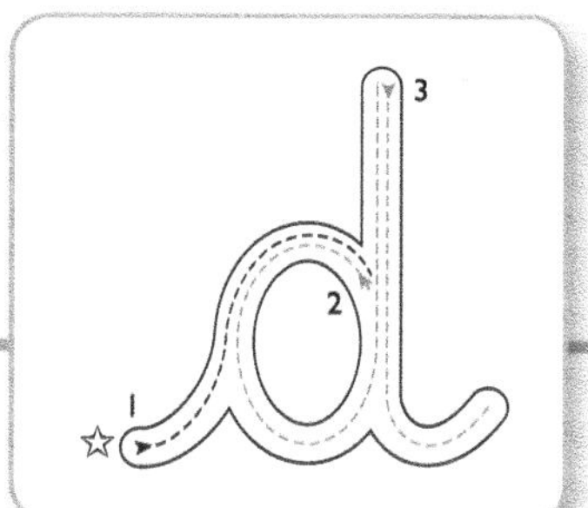

Write over each d on the line here.
Start at the ☆.

Now practise writing the letter d.

Dinosaurs dancing daintily.

How many times is d used in the sentence?

Practise writing over the letter d in these words.

do   dog   edge   hid

do   dog   edge   hid

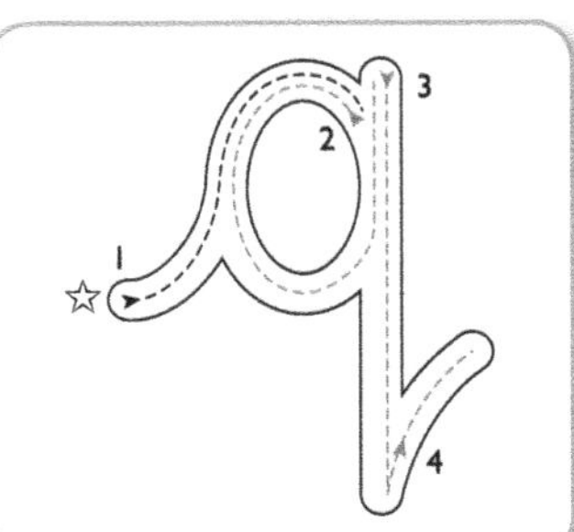

Write over each q on the line here.
Start at the ☆.

Now practise writing the letter q.

The Queen queues quietly.

How many times is q used in the sentence? 

Practise writing over the letter q in these words.

quit quack quiet liquid

quit quack quiet liquid

23 Practising small letters

c o a

Write each of the letters on the three lines below.
Start at the ☆.

☆ c

☆ o

☆ a

Now practise writing the three letters and others
again by writing over the grey letters in each
of the words below.

care care oats oats

acorn acorn blame blame

roam roam closed closed

ape ape orange orange

Practising small letters

Write each of the letters on the three lines below.
Start at the ☆.

Now practise writing the three letters and others
again by writing over the grey letters in each
of the words below.

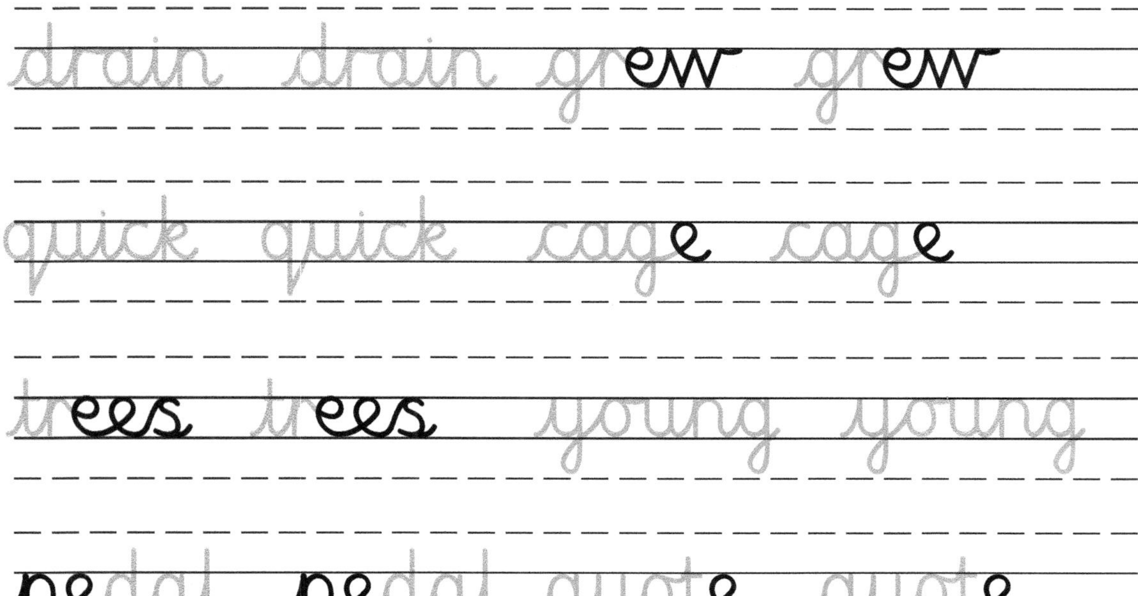

Small letters

Write over each _p_ on the line here.
Start at the ☆.

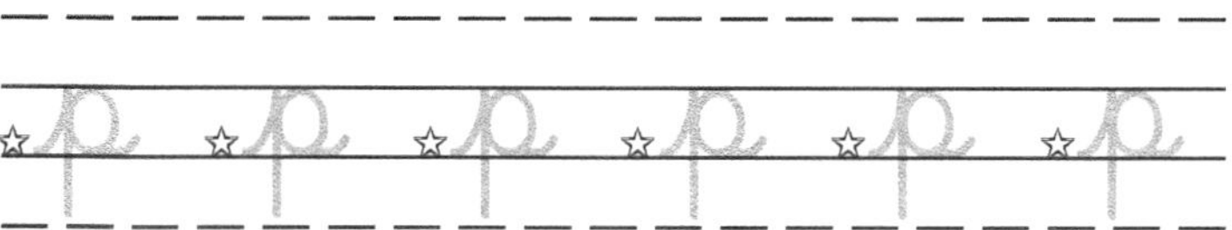

Now practise writing the letter _p_ .

How many times is **p** used in the sentence? 

Practise writing over the letter _p_ in these words.

pet put pull rope top chip

pet put pull rope top chip

Small letters

Write over each _ℓ_ on the line here.
Start at the ☆.

Now practise writing the letter _ℓ_.

Elaine eats eleven eggs.

How many times is _ℓ_ used in the sentence?

Practise writing over the letter _ℓ_ in these words.

eat   end   over   see   send

eat   end   over   see   send

Small letters

Write over each _s_ on the line here.
Start at the ☆.

Now practise writing the letter _s_ .

A sailing ship at sea.

How many times is _s_ used in the sentence?

Practise writing over the letter _s_ in these words.

so say sell house kiss

so say sell house kiss

Small letters

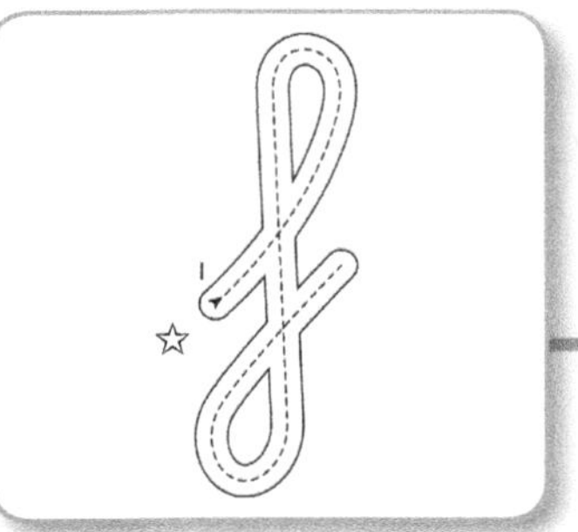

Write over each f on the line here.
Start at the ☆.

Now practise writing the letter f .

How many times is f used in the sentence?

Practise writing over the letter f in these words.

fin fly for raft if tiff

fin fly for raft if tiff

Small letters

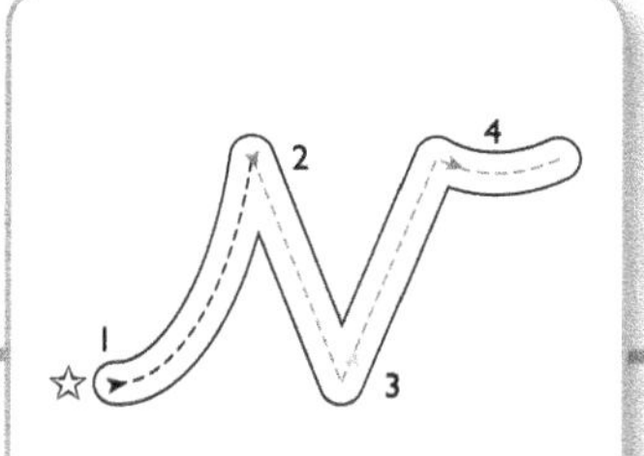

Write over each _n_ on the line here.
Start at the ☆.

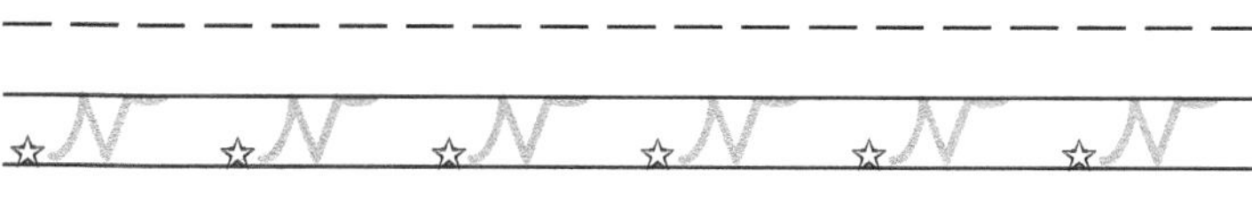

Now practise writing the letter _n_.

Five movers in a van.

How many times is _n_ used in the sentence? ▢

Practise writing over the letter _n_ in these words.

nain nery ever cover wave

nain nery ever cover wave

30 Small letters

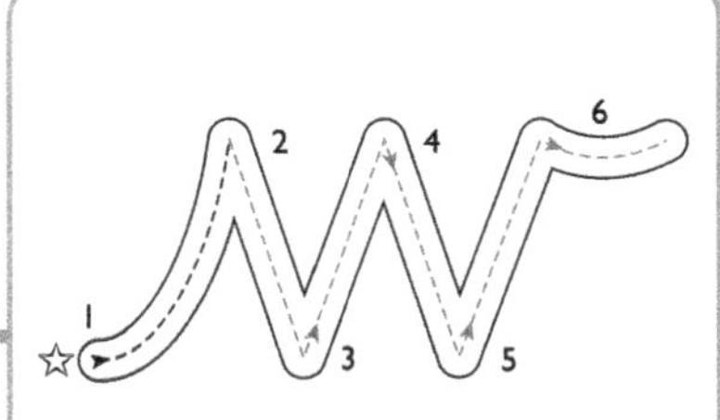

Write over each 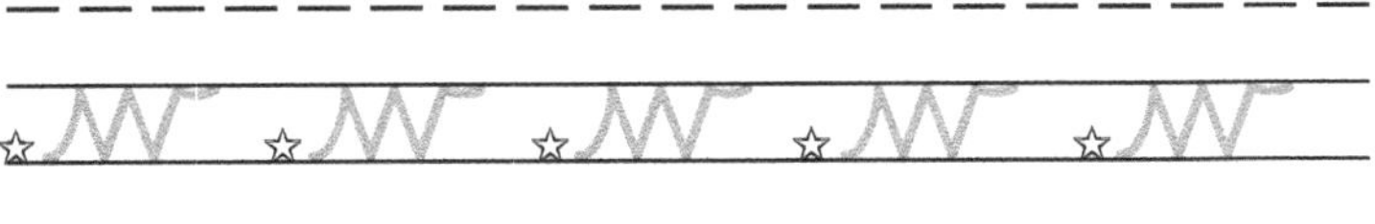 on the line here. Start at the ☆.

Now practise writing the letter ⋏⋏.

How many times is ⋏⋏ used in the sentence? 

Practise writing over the letter ⋏⋏ in these words.

we   why   when   two   bow

we   why   when   two   bow

31 Small letters

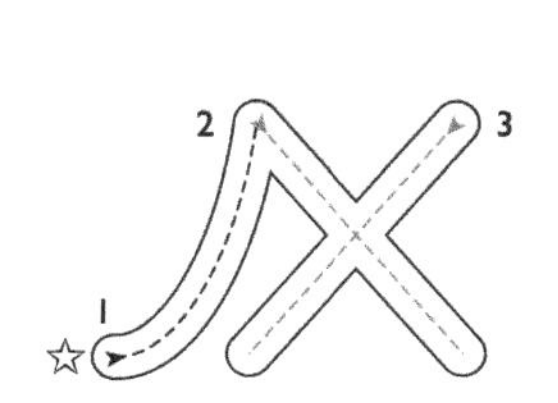

Write over each ✗ on the line here.
Start at the ☆.

Now practise writing the letter ✗ .

Six foxes in boxes.

How many times is ✗ used in the sentence?

Practise writing over the letter ✗ in these words.

fix   mix   axe   flex   coax

fix   mix   axe   flex   coax

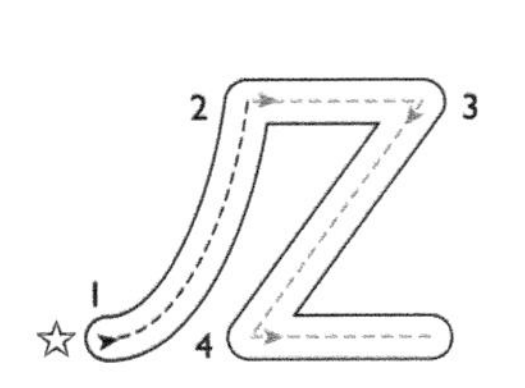

Write over each *z* on the line here.
Start at the ☆.

Now practise writing the letter *z* .

Dozy zebras in the zoo.

How many times is *z* used in the sentence?

Practise writing over the letter *z* in these words.

zip zero glaze buzz fizz

zip zero glaze buzz fizz

Practising small letters

Write each of the letters on the three lines below.
Start at the ☆.

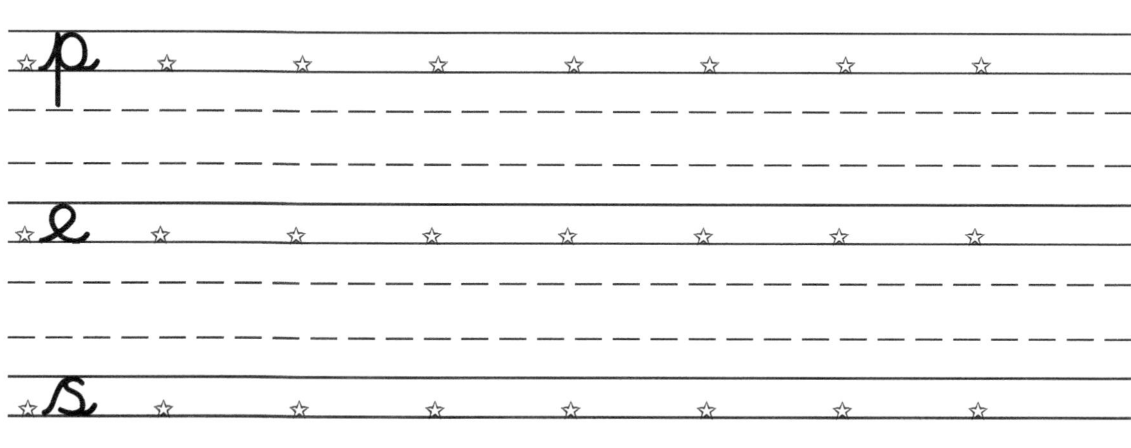

Now practise writing the three letters and others
again by writing over the grey letters in each
of the words below.

Practising small letters

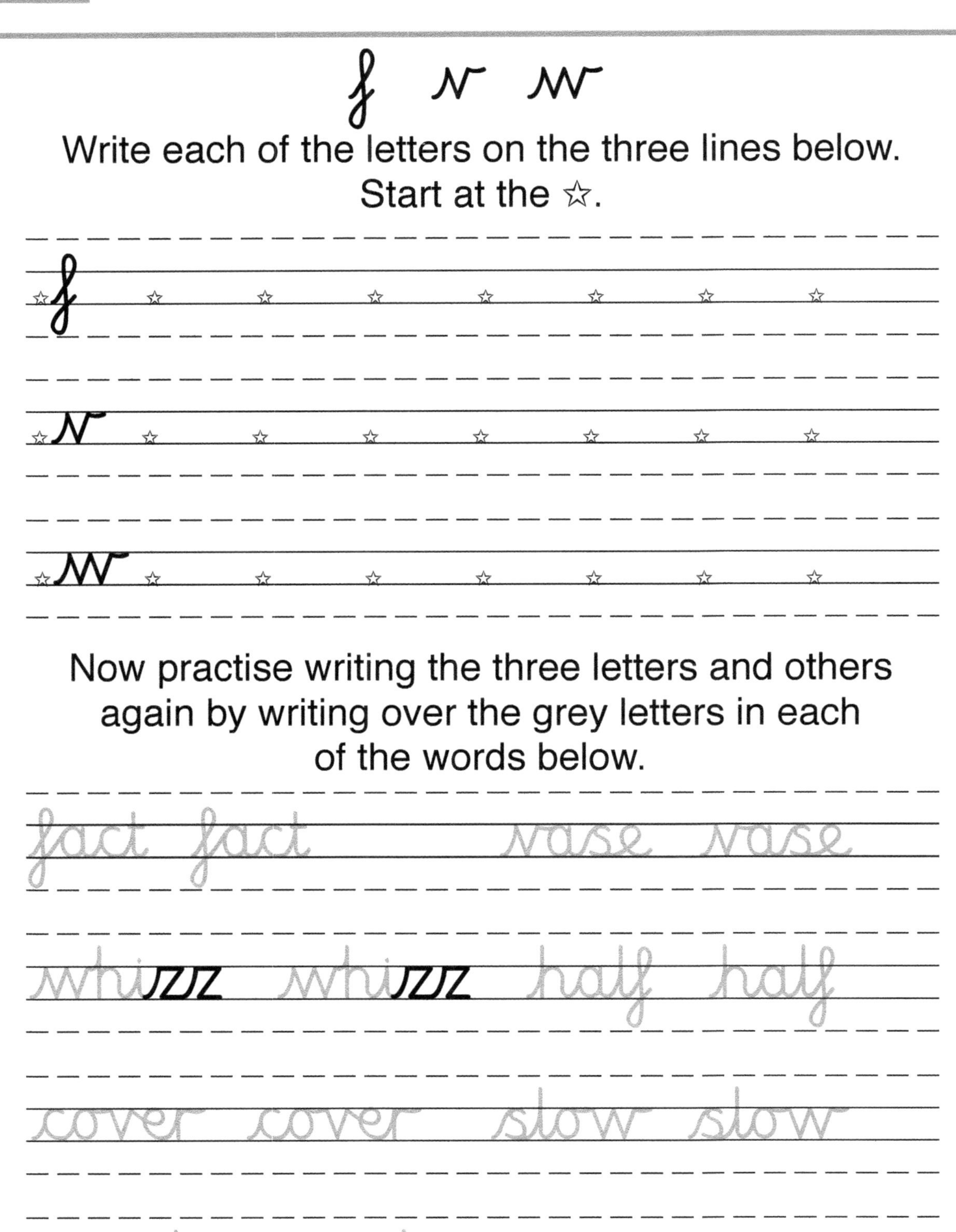

Write each of the letters on the three lines below.
Start at the ☆.

Now practise writing the two letters and others again by writing over the grey letters in each of the words below.

wax wax zebra zebra

mixed mixed lazy lazy

boxer boxer puzzle puzzle

pixie pixie buzz buzz

Spot the small letters

Small letters can be written in many different styles, which can make them look like other letters. In the boxes, draw a line between each capital letter and the correct small letters.

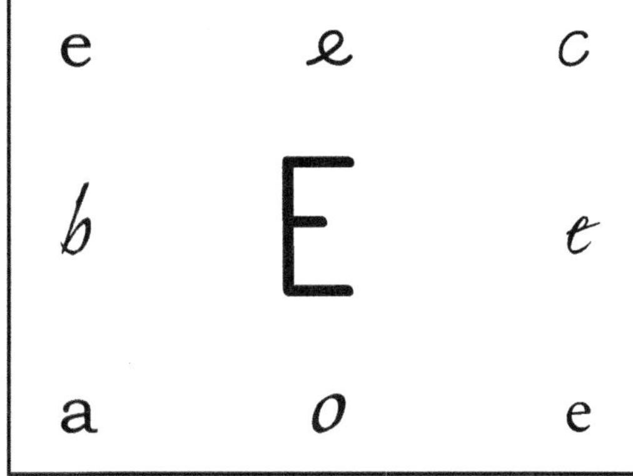

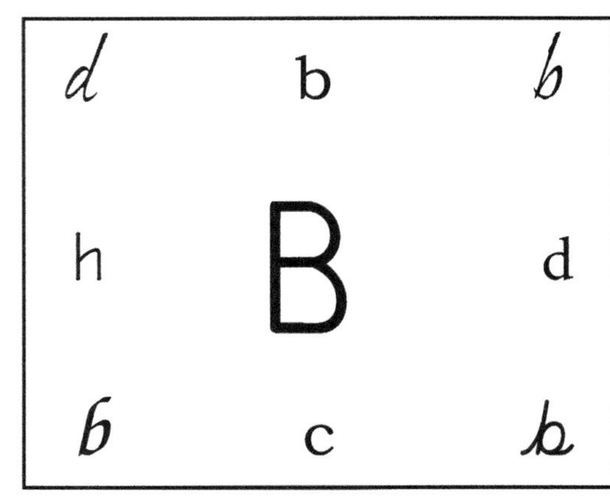

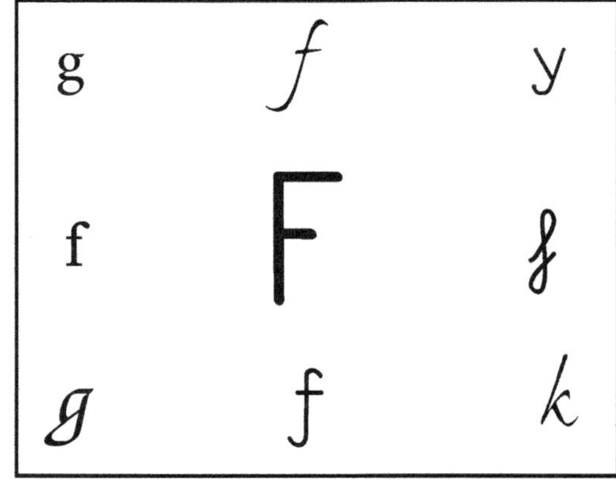

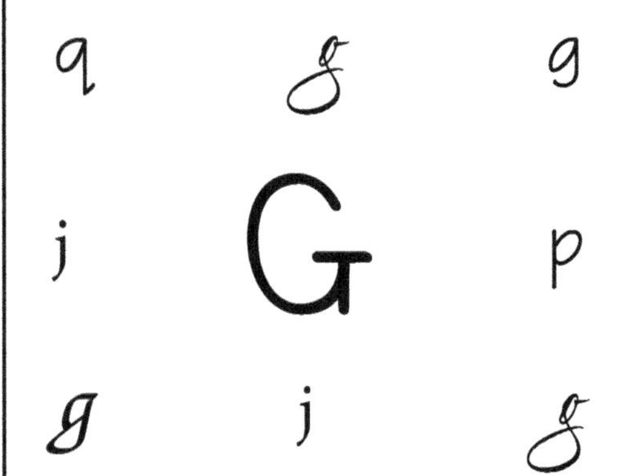

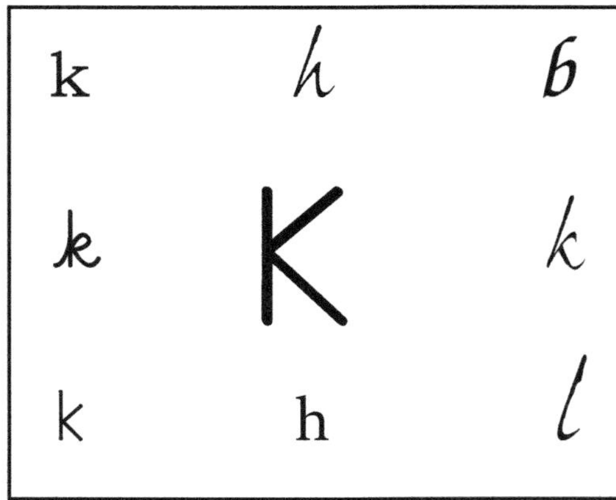

37 Spot the small letters

Small letters can be written in many different styles,
which can make them look like other letters.
In the boxes, draw a line between each capital
letter and the correct small letters.

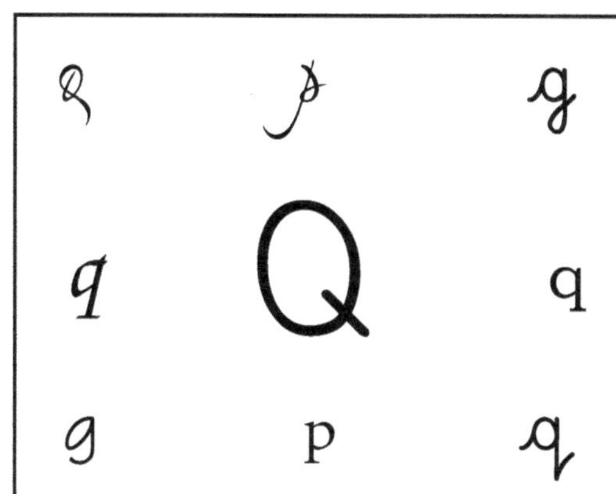

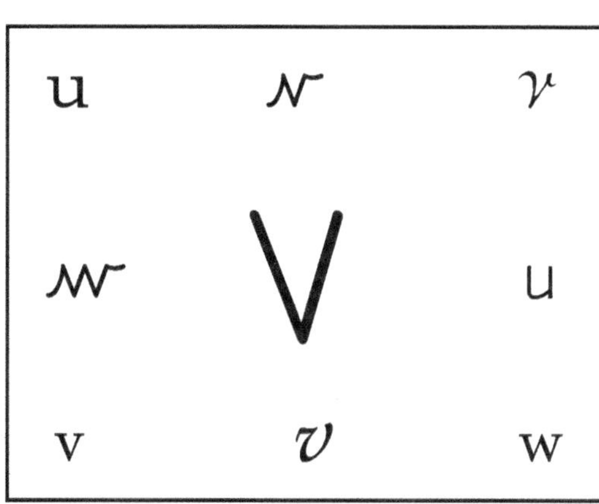

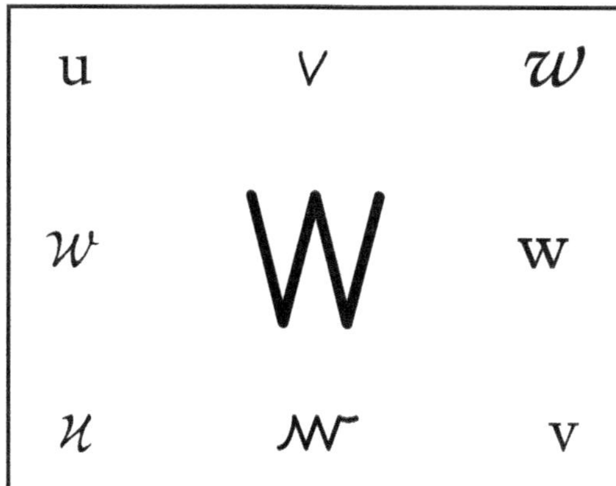

38 Think of a word

Can you write a word beginning with each
of the letters in the alphabet?
Some have been done for you.

a is for apple

b is for b

c is for c

d is for d

e is for egg

f is for fish

g is for g

h is for h

i is for insect

j is for j

k is for kids

l is for l

m is for m

n is for n

o is for o

p is for p

q is for queen

r is for r

s is for s

t is for t

u is for umbrella

v is for very

w is for w

x is for x-ray

y is for y

z is for z

Rhyming words

Write each of the words below. Start at the ☆.
When you have finished, read the words
aloud to your partner.

☆lit

☆bit

☆hit

☆sit

☆wit

☆fit

☆grit

Rhyming words

Write each of the words below. Start at the ☆.
When you have finished, read the words
aloud to your partner.

hill

pill

will

mill

grill

fill

bill

Rhyming words

Write each of the words below. Start at the ☆.
When you have finished, read the words
aloud to your partner.

bin

tin

grin

fin

win

din

pin

Rhyming words

Write each of the words below. Start at the ☆.
When you have finished, read the words
aloud to your partner.

☆tip

☆rip

☆whip

☆zip

☆pip

☆drip

☆grip

Rhyming words

Write each of the words below. Start at the ☆.
When you have finished, read the words
aloud to your partner.

lick

kick

stick

thick

brick

flick

pick

Rhyming words

Write each of the words below. Start at the ☆.
When you have finished, read the words
aloud to your partner.

wing

ring

sting

sing

fling

bring

king

Rhyming words

Write each of the words below. Start at the ☆.
When you have finished, read the words
aloud to your partner.

dig

big

pig

wig

fig

twig

rig

Handwriting check 1:
"Jack and Jill"

Write this well-known rhyme in your
best handwriting. When you have finished,
read it aloud to your partner.

Jack and Jill went up the hill

To fetch a pail of water;

Jack fell down and broke his crown,

And Jill came tumbling after.

Handwriting check 2: "Hey, Diddle, Diddle!"

Write this well-known rhyme in your best handwriting. When you have finished, read it aloud to your partner.

Hey, diddle, diddle!

The cat and the fiddle,

The cow jumped over the moon;

The little dog laughed

To see such fun,

And the dish ran away with the spoon.

ab

Practise writing the *ab* letter join.

ab ab ab ab ab ab ab

Practise writing *ab* on its own.

Join *ab* to these letters to make words.

c   f   t   sl

Add *ab* to complete these two words.

st   le   t   let

Choose four words to practise writing again.

Building words

ack

Practise writing the *ack* letter join.

ack   ack   ack   ack   ack   ack

Practise writing *ack* on its own.

Join *ack* to these letters to make words.

b   h   s   bl

Add *ack* to complete these two words.

t   ing   st   ed

Choose four words to practise writing again.

ad

Practise writing the *ad* letter join.

ad   ad   ad   ad   ad   ad   ad

Practise writing *ad* on its own.

Join *ad* to these letters to make words.

d   m   s   gl

Add *ad* to complete these three words.

d   dy   l   le   s   dle

Choose four words to practise writing again.

Handwriting check 3:
Silly sentences

Write each of these silly sentences
in your best handwriting.

Raggedy Maggy drags Barry's fat cat.

The black sack sat on Sally's saddle.

How many times does the letter a appear
in the two silly sentences?

How many double letters are there
in the two silly sentences?

Handwriting check 4:
"Humpty Dumpty"

Write this well-known rhyme
in your best handwriting.

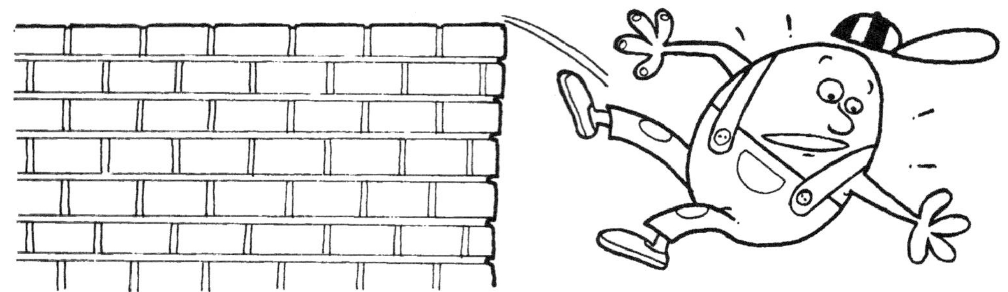

Humpty Dumpty sat on a wall,
Humpty Dumpty had a great fall.
All the King's horses and all the King's men
Couldn't put Humpty together again.

ag

Practise writing the *ag* letter join.

ag ag ag ag ag ag ag

Practise writing *ag* on its own.

Join *ag* to these letters to make words.

b   g   t   fl

Add *ag* to complete these two words.

h   gle   t   ged

Choose four words to practise writing again.

 Building words

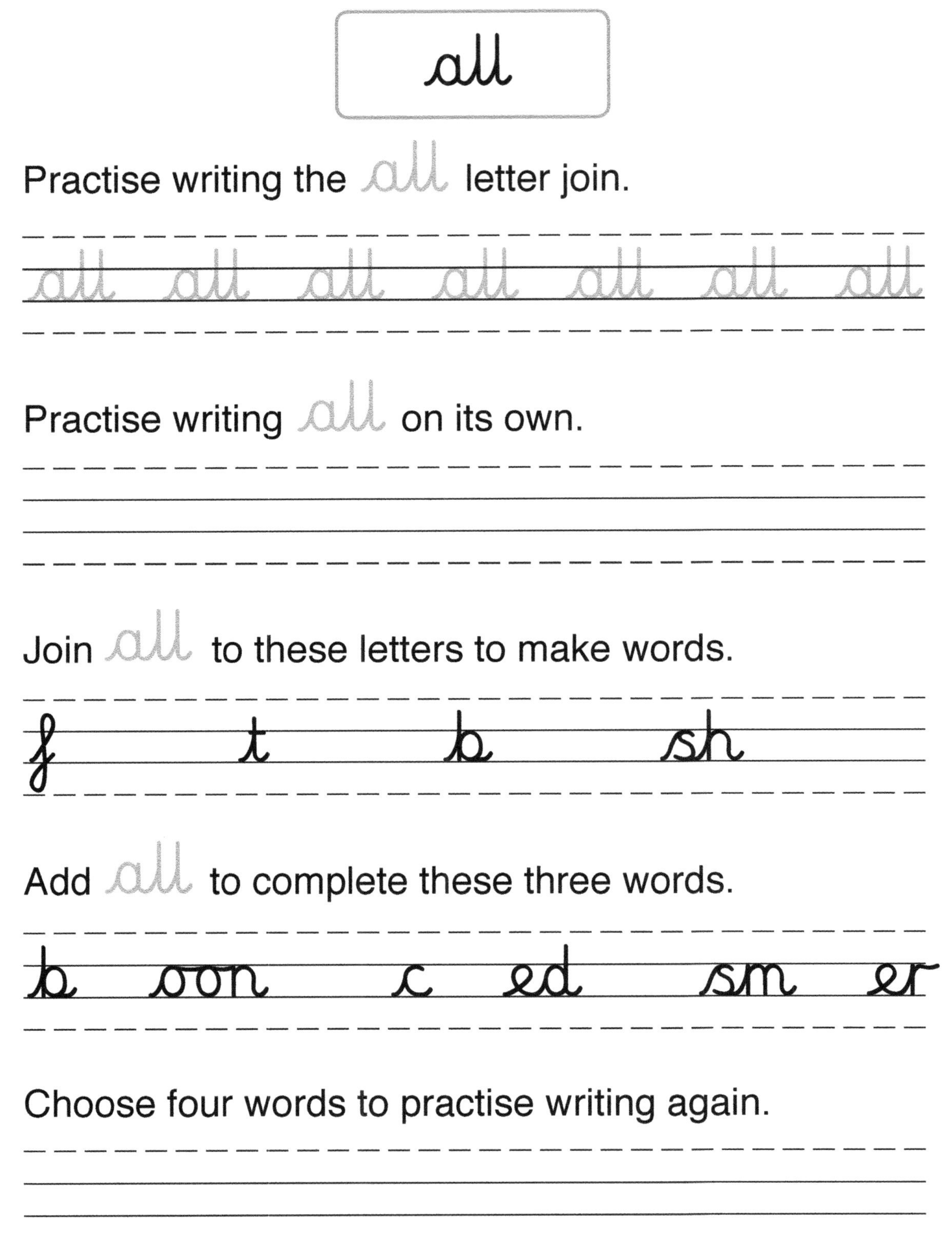

Practise writing the *all* letter join.

Practise writing *all* on its own.

Join *all* to these letters to make words.

f   t   b   sh

Add *all* to complete these three words.

b   oon   c   ed   sm   er

Choose four words to practise writing again.

Building words

am

Practise writing the *am* letter join.

am   am   am   am   am   am

Practise writing *am* on its own.

Join *am* to these letters to make words.

h   j   d   sl

Add *am* to complete these three words.

sh   e   h   mer   l   e

Choose four words to practise writing again.

Building words

amp

Practise writing the amp letter join.

Practise writing amp on its own.

Join amp to these letters to make words.

c____ l____ d____ st____

Add amp to complete these three words.

c____ ed d____ en h____ er

Choose four words to practise writing again.

an

Practise writing the *an* letter join.

an an an an an an an

Practise writing *an* on its own.

Join *an* to these letters to make words.

c   f   b   th

Add *an* to complete these three words.

pl e   m   ner   t   ned

Choose four words to practise writing again.

Building words

and

Practise writing the *and* letter join.

and and and and and

Practise writing *and* on its own.

Join *and* to these letters to make words.

b   h   s   l

Add *and* to complete these three words.

s   ed   s   y   p   a

Choose four words to practise writing again.

Building words

ank

Practise writing the _ank_ letter join.

ank ank ank ank ank

Practise writing _ank_ on its own.

Join _ank_ to these letters to make words.

b s t sp

Add _ank_ to complete these three words.

b er pl s th ed

Choose four words to practise writing again.

Building words

ar

Practise writing the *ar* letter join.

Practise writing *ar* on its own.

Join *ar* to these letters to make words.

c   f   b   j

Add *ar* to complete these three words.

e   af   st

Choose four words to practise writing again.

Handwriting check 5:
"Higgledy Piggledy my black hen"

Write this well-known rhyme
in your best handwriting.

Higgledy Piggledy my black hen,
She lays eggs for gentlemen.
Gentlemen come every day,
To see what my black hen will lay.

ash

Practise writing the *ash* letter join.

ash ash ash ash ash

Practise writing *ash* on its own.

Join *ash* to these letters to make words.

b   d   c   fl

Add *ash* to complete these three words.

spl ed   d ing   b ed

Choose four words to practise writing again.

63 Building words

atch

Practise writing the atch letter join.

atch atch atch atch atch

Practise writing atch on its own.

Join atch to these letters to make words.

c   l   m   p

Add atch to complete these three words.

c   er th   ed h   ing

Choose four words to practise writing again.

Building words

aw

Practise writing the *aw* letter join.

Practise writing *aw* on its own.

Join *aw* to these letters to make words.

j   p   s   d

Add *aw* to complete these three words.

s   ing   l   n   th   ed

Choose four words to practise writing again.

ay

Practise writing the *ay* letter join.

Practise writing *ay* on its own.

Join *ay* to these letters to make words.

d　　p　　s　　st

Add *ay* to complete these three words.

pl　time　　d　　rel　ed

Choose four words to practise writing again.

Don't forget the punctuation! – ? " " , . !

Write these sentences on another sheet of paper, making sure to add the missing capital letters, full stops and any other punctuation required.

Think about this!

All the names should start with a capital letter.
Which words are abbreviations?
Where should speech marks go?
What punctuation mark should be added at the end of the final sentence?

1. mr robinson is coming to tea on tuesday

2. mrs brown said get ready for your p e lesson

3. i had a birthday card addressed to miss jane long

4. my cat chloe is washing her whiskers

5. bill said are you coming to watch liverpool play

Building words

et

Practise writing the *et* letter join.

et et et et et et et et et

Practise writing *et* on its own.

Join *et* to these letters to make words.

m   j   s

Add *et* to complete these three words.

l ter   p ted   b ter

Choose four words to practise writing again.

 Building words

ell

Practise writing the *ell* letter join.

ell   ell   ell   ell   ell   ell   ell

Practise writing *ell* on its own.

Join *ell* to these letters to make words.

b   f   t   sh

Add *ell* to complete these three words.

m   ow   j   y   s   ing

Choose four words to practise writing again.

Building words

en

Practise writing the *en* letter join.

en en en en en en en

Practise writing *en* on its own.

Join *en* to these letters to make words.

h   m   p   t

Add *en* to complete these three words.

g eral   p cil   t th

Choose four words to practise writing again.

Building words

est

Practise writing the *est* letter join.

est est est est est est

Practise writing *est* on its own.

Join *est* to these letters to make words.

n   *b*   *r*   *qu*

Add *est* to complete these three words.

ch   *y*   *j*   *er*   *t*   *ed*

Choose four words to practise writing again.

Building words

ick

Practise writing the *ick* letter join.

ick ick ick ick ick ick

Practise writing *ick* on its own.

Join *ick* to these letters to make words.

t   s   t   st

Add *ick* to complete these three words.

d   ed   p   s   t   le

Choose four words to practise writing again.

Building words

iff

Practise writing the *iff* letter join.

Practise writing *iff* on its own.

Join *iff* to these letters to make words.

b   m   t   wh

Add *iff* to complete these two words.

cl s   st en

Choose four words to practise writing again.

Building words

ig

Practise writing the *ig* letter join.

ig ig ig ig ig ig ig ig

Practise writing *ig* on its own.

Join *ig* to these letters to make words.

b   *d*   *p*   *f*

Add *ig* to complete these three words.

b gest   *d ger*   *g gle*

Choose four words to practise writing again.

Handwriting check 6:
Silly sentences

Write each of these silly sentences
in your best handwriting.

Send ten men to rescue Ken and Debbie.

Three green trees shed their leaves.

How many times does the letter *e* appear
in the two silly sentences?

How many double letters are there
in the two silly sentences?

Building words

in

Practise writing the *in* letter join.

in in in in in in in in

Practise writing *in* on its own.

Join *in* to these letters to make words.

f   p   t   sh

Add *in* to complete these three words.

d ner   t ned   warn g

Choose four words to practise writing again.

ing

Practise writing the *ing* letter join.

ing ing ing ing ing ing

Practise writing *ing* on its own.

Join *ing* to these letters to make words.

p   s   z   k

Add *ing* to complete these three words.

k dom   s ing   th s

Choose four words to practise writing again.

Building words

ip

Practise writing the *ip* letter join.

ip   ip   ip   ip   ip   ip   ip   ip

Practise writing *ip* on its own.

Join *ip* to these letters to make words.

d   h   l   wh

Add *ip* to complete these three words.

ch_s   sl_ped   n_per

Choose four words to practise writing again.

 Building words

it

Practise writing the *it* letter join.

it it it it it it it it it

Practise writing *it* on its own.

Join *it* to these letters to make words.

b   s   p   st

Add *it* to complete these three words.

b ing   k ten   wh e

Choose four words to practise writing again.

Handwriting check 7:
Silly sentences

Write each of these silly sentences
in your best handwriting.

King Griff had a stiff quiff.

King Biff the Bigger giggled and got better.

How many times does the letter *i* appear
in the two silly sentences?

How many double letters are there
in the two silly sentences?

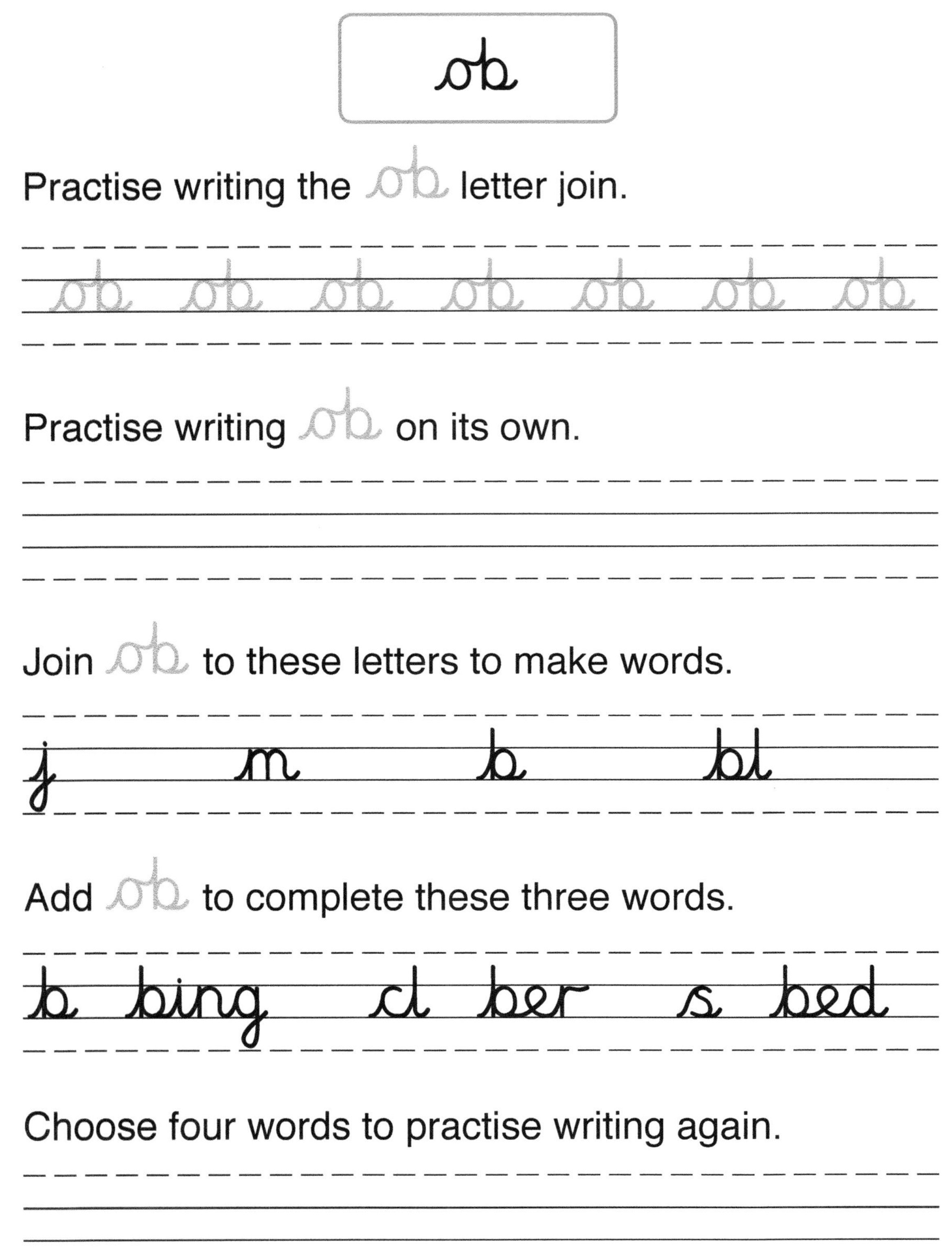

ob

Practise writing the ob letter join.

Practise writing ob on its own.

Join ob to these letters to make words.

j   m   b   bl

Add ob to complete these three words.

b bing   d ber   s bed

Choose four words to practise writing again.

Building words

ock

Practise writing the *ock* letter join.

ock   ock   ock   ock   ock   ock

Practise writing *ock* on its own.

Join *ock* to these letters to make words.

t   d   s   fl

Add *ock* to complete these three words.

bl ed   cl s   sh ed

Choose four words to practise writing again.

og

Practise writing the *og* letter join.

Practise writing *og* on its own.

Join *og* to these letters to make words.

b   c   d   sl

Add *og* to complete these three words.

f gy   j ged   l s

Choose four words to practise writing again.

83 Building words

op

Practise writing the *op* letter join.

Practise writing *op* on its own.

Join *op* to these letters to make words.

c   h   t   sh

Add *op* to complete these three words.

fl_s   st_es   st_ped

Choose four words to practise writing again.

Building words

ot

Practise writing the *ot* letter join.

ot ot ot ot ot ot ot ot

Practise writing *ot* on its own.

Join *ot* to these letters to make words.

d   *h*   *j*   *sp*

Add *ot* to complete these three words.

d ted   *l tery*   *m her*

Choose four words to practise writing again.

Building words

ub

Practise writing the *ub* letter join.

ub ub ub ub ub ub ub

Practise writing *ub* on its own.

Join *ub* to these letters to make words.

c   p   t   st

Add *ub* to complete these three words.

cl bed   st by   b ble

Choose four words to practise writing again.

uck

Practise writing the *uck* letter join.

uck   uck   uck   uck   uck

Practise writing *uck* on its own.

Join *uck* to these letters to make words.

d   m   s   st

Add *uck* to complete these three words.

d   ed   l   y   pl   ed

Choose four words to practise writing again.

Handwriting check 8:
"Little Tommy Tucker"

Write this well-known rhyme
in your best handwriting.

Little Tommy Tucker,
Sings for his supper.
What shall we get him?
Brown bread and butter!

Building words

ug

Practise writing the ug letter join.

Practise writing ug on its own.

Join ug to these letters to make words.

b   d   t   th

Add ug to complete these three words.

m ger   pl ged   th s

Choose four words to practise writing again.

Building words

um

Practise writing the *um* letter join.

um um um um um um

Practise writing *um* on its own.

Join *um* to these letters to make words.

g   h   s   ch

Add *um* to complete these three words.

th   bs   m   my   n   b

Choose four words to practise writing again.

90 Building words

un

Practise writing the _un_ letter join.

Practise writing _un_ on its own.

Join _un_ to these letters to make words.

b   n   f   st

Add _un_ to complete these three words.

f   ny   g   s   s   shine

Choose four words to practise writing again.

Building words

ut

Practise writing the *ut* letter join.

ut ut ut ut ut ut ut ut

Practise writing *ut* on its own.

Join *ut* to these letters to make words.

c ___   h ___   p ___   sh ___

Add *ut* to complete these three words.

b ___ ter   g ___ ter   n ___ ty

Choose four words to practise writing again.

Handwriting check 9:
Silly sentences

Write each of these silly sentences
in your best handwriting.

The top cop stopped the rotten robber.

Flopsy mopped the sloppy slops.

How many times does the letter o appear
in the two silly sentences?

How many double letters are there
in the two silly sentences?

Handwriting check 10:
Silly sentences

Write each of these silly sentences
in your best handwriting.

Bugs Bunny has a funny tummy.

The mucky truck missed the lucky duck.

How many times does the letter u appear
in the two silly sentences?

How many double letters are there
in the two silly sentences?

Handwriting check 11:
"The Boy in the Barn"

Write this well-known rhyme
in your best handwriting.

A little boy went into a barn
And lay down on some hay.
An owl came out, and flew about,
And the little boy ran away.